THE INSTRUCTION WRITER'S GUIDE:

HOW TO EXPLAIN HOW TO DO *ANYTHING!*

By

Marilyn Haight

The Instruction Writer's Guide:
How to Explain How to Do Anything

Copyright © 2004 by Marilyn Haight

ISBN 978-0-9800390-2-3
Library of Congress Control Number: 2008922334

Published by:
Worded Write Publishing
20403 N. Lake Pleasant Rd.
Suite #117-150
Peoria, AZ 85382-9707
Phone: (623) 825-3845
Web: http://www.wordedwrite.com

Worded

Write

Published February 2008

Table of Contents

Introduction.. vi
1. Allow Enough Time...1
2. Collect and Organize Reference Materials 11
3. Observe a Worker and Take Notes 15
4. Replace Jargon 20
5. Introduce Your Instructions 23
6. Introduce New Language 26
7. Use Short Sentences and Common Words....................29
8. Use Abbreviations and Acronyms Carefully 32
9. Speak Directly to Your Readers..............................35
10. Be Positive and Focused 36
11. Be Exact 39
12. Be Consistent 44
  1. Names..44
  2. Abbreviations and Symbols 45
  3. Acronyms 45
  4. Whole Numbers- Non-financial............................46
  5. Whole Numbers Less Than 10 47
  6. Whole Numbers of 7 Digits or More 47
  7. Zero 48
  8. Fractions..48
  9. Whole Numbers with Fractions 48
  10. Decimal Fractions 49
  11. Quantity and Measurement Statements....................49
  12. Financial Values...50
13. Be Easy on the Eyes..51
  1. Set Wide Side Margins 51
  2. Set Large Top and Bottom Margins........................52
  3. Present Steps on the Same Page...........................53
  4. Indent Paragraphs..53
  5. Separate Paragraphs 53
  6. List Items...54

7. Separate Listed Items 54
8. Center Short Text 55
9. Indent Subordinate Steps 55
10. Use Easy-to-Read Fonts..56
11. Select An Easy-to-Read Print Size..........................56
12. Emphasize Key Words...57
14. Identify Necessary Resources 58
15. Inform Readers of Hazards 59
16. Arrange Steps in Order..61
17. Include Checkpoints at Critical Stages 64
18. Begin Action Steps with "Do" and "Degree" Words.....67
19. Describe People, Locations and Things with "Picture"
Words 70
20. Describe Noises with "Sound" Words 73
21. Describe Flavors with "Taste" Words........................75
22. Describe Textures with "Touch" Words 76
23. Describe Odors with "Smell" Words 77
24. Illustrate Your Instructions 78
    1. Photographs and Drawings 80
    2. Four-Box or Quadrant Charts 83
    3. Combination or Matrix Tables 84
    4. Flowcharts...86
    5. Graphs and Charts...87
    6. Worksheets..89
25. Guide Readers in Solving Problems 91
26. Refer to Additional Information 93
27. Describe "The End"..95
28. Test Your Instructions..97
29. Revise and Release Your Instructions......................101
Appendix A: Vague Expressions to Avoid 104
Appendix B: "Do" and "Degree" Words..........................105
Appendix C: "Picture" Words...107
Appendix D: "Sound" Words...109

Appendix E: "Taste," "Touch" and "Smell" Words 111
Appendix F: "On-Screen" Instructions 112

Introduction

This publication answers the question:

"How can I write instructions that my readers will clearly understand?"

This step-by-step guide teaches you how to write an explanation of how to do *anything*. That's right, *anything*! Whether the task involves physical activities, like assembly or setup, or mental activities, like problem-solving or learning, this publication can help you write excellent instructions!

This is *not* a guide for writing complete learning programs. There are plenty of books available to teach you how to do that. But those books don't teach you how to choose and arrange words to guide readers as they perform a task. This publication does.

Who needs this publication? Product managers, administrators, business managers, teachers, technical writers, trainers, web-content writers and anyone else who writes instructions. Why? Because, when you write instructions, your goal is to help your readers accomplish a task quickly and successfully. This publication shows you how to do that.

The Instruction Writer's Guide: How to Explain How to Do Anything can be used as a stand-alone learning tool, a reference guide or a textbook supplement for students of Education, Instructional Design and Technical Writing.

1. Allow Enough Time

Whether you're writing a brief explanation or a lengthy manual, it almost always takes longer than you think it will to write good instructions. If you're an experienced instruction writer, you can estimate the time you need based on past experience with similar projects. But what if you've never written instructions, or what if you're attempting a larger project? How can you estimate how much time you'll need?

This chapter walks you through a process for doing just that. It produces an estimate that will be accurate almost 95% of the time within a 10% range. How do I know this? Because I've tested it time and again over more than 15 years.

Your estimate may seem high at first, but trust it. Even if your estimate is high, it's much less stressful to correct an over-estimate than an under-estimate!

Follow the "Time Estimate Worksheet" on the next page as you read through this chapter. Permission is granted to copy this worksheet one time for the purpose of learning this method. As an alternative to copying the worksheet, use a lined sheet of paper and number rows from 1 through 11.

1

Time Estimate Worksheet				
Step	**Activity**	**Est. Hours**	**Total Hours**	**Total Days**
1	Time to learn to perform the task:			
2	Time to locate reference materials:			
3	Time to read reference materials:			
4	Time to get people to agree to be observed:			
5	Time to observe and take notes:			
6	Number of times you will observe someone performing the task: _____			
7	Multiply the time in step 5 by the number of observations in step 6.			
8	Add the estimated hours entered on lines 1 through 5 and 7:	**Sum:**		
9	Multiply the sum in step 8 by the number "5" (round up to a whole number):			
10	Number of hours you will spend writing instructions each day: _____			
11	Divide the "Total Hours" in step 9 by the number of hours in step 10 (round up to the half or whole hour):			
Enter all values as hours in decimal form. For example: 1 ½ hours = 1.5 hours; 75 minutes = 1.25 hours.				

2

Follow these 11 steps to estimate the time you will need to complete your instructions:

1. **Estimate the amount of time you will need to learn the task.**

    - Enter your estimate in the "Estimated Hours" column.

    - If you are familiar with task, enter "0".

    - If you are unfamiliar with the task, **guess** how long it will take to learn it. Base your answer on how long it took the last time you learned something equally difficult. Trust your gut or your intuition—you will correct for it later.

2. **Estimate the time required to locate and obtain reference materials.**

    - Put this number in the "Estimated Hours" column.

    - Enter "0" if you do not need reference materials.

    - If you need reference materials, guess the amount of time you will need to locate them, including research and travel time.

3. **Estimate the time required to read reference materials.**

    - Enter your estimate in the "Estimated Hours" column.

    - Enter "0" if you do not need to read.

- If you plan to read, base your answer on how long it took the last time you read technical material of the same length. Or, triple the amount of time it takes to read entertaining material of the same length.

4. **Estimate the time you will need to get experts to agree to be observed as they perform the task.**

  - Enter your estimate in the "Estimated Hours" column. (This step helps you capture details that you might overlook or take for granted due to familiarity See Chapter 3, *Observe a Worker*, for details).

  - If you plan to observe yourself at the task, enter "0".

  - If you plan to observe others, consider the amount of time required to reach them (by phone; e-mail; in person; letter) and to explain your purpose for wanting to observe them.

5. **Estimate the amount of time you will need to observe the task in progress and take notes** (see Chapter 3, *Observe a Worker*, for details).

  - Enter this number in the "Estimated Hours" column.

  - If you plan to observe yourself as you perform the task, multiply the time it usually takes by "3."

  - If you plan to observe others, ask them how much time they need to perform the task.

Average their responses and double the average to allow time for you to interrupt and ask questions.

6. Enter the number of times you plan to observe the task as it is being performed.

- Enter your estimate on the line provided in the "Activity" column.

- Enter at least "1" to allow for observing yourself or someone else (details are explained in Chapter 3, *Observe a Worker*).

- If there are different ways to perform the task, count how many ways there are and plan to observe at least once for each; enter your total.

7. Estimate the amount of time you will need to learn the task.

- Multiply the number on line 5, "Time to observe and take notes," by the number of observations you entered on line 6. Enter your result in the "Estimated Hours" column on line 7. For example:

- If you entered "3.5" on Line 5 (Time to observe and take notes) and

- If you entered "3" on Line 6 (Number of times you will observe), then you would enter "10.5" on Line 7 (3.5 x 3).

8. Estimate the amount of time you will need to study the task.

- Add the numbers you entered in the "Estimated Hours" column for lines 1 through 5 and 7.

- Enter the result in the "Estimated Hours" column on line 8.

9. Multiply the sum on line 8 by the number "5" and round up to a whole number.

- Enter the result in the "Total Hours" column. For example:

- If you entered "17" on Line 8, you would enter "85" on Line 9 (17 x 5).

- This factor-of-five multiplication step allows time for other activities, such as: editing as you write; re-reading your notes; verifying information; re-enacting parts of the task for clarification; asking questions; reading, analyzing and including the comments of others who critique your drafts; and interruptions that cause you to have to retrace steps.

(NOTE: If you are like most people, you doubt this step and think the factor-of-five is too high. Only experience will convince you or anyone to whom you are accountable that this method works.)

Step 9 helped you calculate how many total hours you will need to write your instructions. Steps 10 and 11 help you convert those hours into workdays.

10. Determine the number of hours you will work on this project each day.

- Enter your answer on the line provided in the "Activity" column for step 10.

- If you typically work an 8-hour day, other responsibilities may keep you from working on your instruction-writing project. Determine how many hours each day you will *actually* devote to this project.

11. Determine the actual number of workdays required.

- Divide the "Total Hours" you entered in step 9 by the number of hours you entered in step 10. Enter your answer in the "Total Days" column.

- This is the estimated number of actual workdays you will need to write your instructions.

Examples of completed "Time Estimate Worksheets" are provided on the next two pages. Example A illustrates an estimate made by someone who is *un*familiar with faucets and who plans to write instructions for replacing one. Example B illustrates an estimate for the same project made by an experienced plumber who is familiar with faucets.

Example A: Instruction Writer _Un_familiar with Task

Time Estimate Worksheet				
Step	**Activity**	**Est. Hours**	**Total Hours**	**Total Days**
1	Time to learn to perform the task:	3.5		
2	Time to locate reference materials:	2.0		
3	Time to read reference materials:	2.0		
4	Time to get people to agree to be observed:	3.0		
5	Time to observe and take notes:	1.0		
6	Number of times you will observe someone performing the task: _2			
7	Multiply the time in step 5 by the number of observations in step 6.	2.0		
8	Add the estimated hours entered on lines 1 through 5 and 7:	**Sum:** **13.5**		
9	Multiply the sum in step 8 by the number "5" (round up to a whole number):		68	
10	Number of hours you will spend writing instructions each day: 6.0			
11	Divide the "Total Hours" in step 9 by the number of hours in step 10 (round up to the half or whole hour):			11.5

Example B: Instruction Writer Familiar with Task

\multicolumn{5}{c}{**Time Estimate Worksheet**}
Step	**Activity**	**Est. Hours**	**Total Hours**	**Total Days**
---	---	---	---	---
1	Time to learn to perform the task:	0		
2	Time to locate reference materials:	0		
3	Time to read reference materials:	0		
4	Time to get people to agree to be observed:	1.0		
5	Time to observe and take notes:	1.0		
6	Number of times you will observe someone performing the task: 1			
7	Multiply the time in step 5 by the number of observations in step 6.	1.0		
8	Add the estimated hours entered on lines 1 through 5 and 7:	**Sum: 3.0**		
9	Multiply the sum in step 8 by the number "5" (round up to a whole number):		15	
10	Number of hours you will spend writing instructions each day: 6.0			
11	Divide the "Total Hours" in step 9 by the number of hours in step 10 (round up to the half or whole hour):			2.5

Step 9 tells you the actual number of hours you will spend writing instructions. You might be inclined to divide that number by the number of days available; however, this figure is likely to be incorrect. It is rare that a workday is dedicated exclusively to one project without interruptions. Steps 10 and 11 take into account that some time may be devoted to other activities during your workdays. These last two steps help you determine a realistic end date by which your work can be completed.

2. Collect and Organize Reference Materials

The instructions for setting up a document in a word processor said: "*Click on the 'Paper Size' tab.*" But there was no "Paper Size" tab. It took me ten minutes to find a screen that allowed paper-size adjustments. I tossed the instructions aside and didn't look at them again.

How can an instruction writer make such a mistake, telling a reader to use something that isn't there? By being poorly prepared and relying on memory or assumption rather than verified information.

We judge products, services and people by the accuracy of their documentation. We learned to do this in grammar school when our papers were returned to us with red correction marks and grades. When the instructions are incorrect, we do the mental equivalent of assigning an "F" to them.

This chapter tells you how to be well prepared. It describes the resources you must have at hand before you begin writing instructions. Follow these guidelines, and you'll be sure to get an "A" from your readers!

11

Physical Resources

#	What To Get	Examples
1	Equipment associated with the task you are writing about	If you are writing instructions for operating a cell phone, make sure you have the model you are writing about in your hand, rather than relying on memory or a picture.
2	References that describe aspects of the task you are writing about, such as books, manuals and data disks	If you are writing a First Aid instruction, get: • First Aid manuals • Dictionaries of Medical Terms
3	Writing books	Helpful references include: • Dictionary • Grammar and spelling guide • Thesaurus

Create an easy-to-reach space in your work area to store these references while you are writing instructions.

Virtual Resources

#	What To Access	Examples
4	Locate Internet web sites that contain valid information about the task you are writing about as well as writing skills, and bookmark them.	Bookmark: http://www.copyright.gov if you are writing instructions about how to copyright. Bookmark: http://www.wordedwrite.com for helpful writing tips.
5	If you work for a large organization that has electronic files, locate Intranet files that contain information relevant to the task.	Bookmark the pathname for local, proprietary information according to your organization's guidelines.
6	Add e-mail addresses to your e-mail address list for subject matter experts you may want to contact.	For example, add: marilyn@wordedwrite.com.

Create a virtual folder in your browser. Give it the name of the task you are writing about. Transfer your bookmarks for valid reference sites into this folder. This will allow you to quickly reference these resources while you are writing.

Be aware that virtual resources may change at any time. Each time you access them, refresh the web page to get the most current version. If you reference virtual resources in your instructions, include the date on which you accessed the information, for example, write: "as accessed on April 15, 2005."

3. Observe a Worker and Take Notes

The instructions said: "*To shred paper, insert into slot on top of unit.*" Okay. Paper inserted. Nothing happens. Now what?

This instruction would have worked for a full-sized sheet of paper, but a narrow sheet would not go through. Here's a case of an instruction writer so familiar with a task that she left out an important detail. Paper must be inserted into the left-hand side of the slot to trigger the switch that starts the motor on this unit. The instruction writer always inserts paper into the left-hand side without thinking about it.

The more familiar you are with a process, the more likely it is that you may overlook a step. How can you be sure you include all of those small, yet important steps? Study. Before you begin writing, watch a capable worker perform the task, ask about all decisions that are made and take notes.

This is the most important step you will perform as an instruction writer. Regardless of how experienced or familiar you are with the task, observe an expert or competent person performing the task and take notes. Describe every action and explain every decision the worker makes. If you cannot observe someone else, perform the task yourself; go slowly and list everything you think and do—one step at a time.

This chapter explains how to conduct an observation of the task you are going to describe in your instructions. You will need something to write on, something to write with and a timer.

#	What To Do	How To Do It
	Steps for Observing	
1	Ask for permission.	Make an appointment
2	Ask for explanations.	Ask workers to explain what they are doing.
3	Notice resources.	Note references and equipment used by the worker.
4	Slow down the action.	Ask workers to slow down if you need time to write all the details.
5	Watch every movement.	Assign a number to every action and write what the worker does.
6	Notice hesitations.	Hesitations may indicate uncertainty, decision-making or problems.
7	Note the time spent on each step.	Use a stop watch or timer you can glance at.
8	Ask questions.	Ask workers why they are doing whatever they are doing and whether there are alternatives. Note their answers, the choices they make, and their reasons.
9	Observe alternative methods.	Ask if there are other ways to perform the task and observe those methods, too.

Following is an example of what your notes might look like if you observed someone turning on a television connected to a cable TV service:

1. *Decide whether to use the manual controls on the television or the remote control unit.*

    -   *You must be physically located at the television to use the manual controls.*

    -   *You may be as far as 20 feet away from the television to use the remote control unit.*

2. *Step 2. Turn on the television using the manual controls:*

    -   *Press the "Power" button on the cable box.*

    -   *Press the "Power" button on the television.*

3. *Turn on the television using the remote control unit (alternative):*

    -   *Locate the "Power" section on the remote control unit (it includes three buttons labeled: TV, VCR, CBL).*

    -   *Aim the remote control unit at the front of the cable box.*

    -   *Press the "CBL" button in the "Power" section of the remote control unit.*

    -   *Press the "TV" button in the "Power" section of the remote control unit.*

- *You are finished with remote control unit.*

4. *Step 4: Verify that the television is on.*

    - *Listen for sound and look for a picture on the screen.*

    - *If you find either of these, then you have successfully turned on the television and you may proceed to Step 5. If the television does not turn on, continue.*

    - *If there is no sound or picture, determine whether power is getting to the television:*

        ◊ *Make sure the television is plugged into an electrical outlet.*

        ◊ *Determine whether a power switch controls the electrical outlet and switch it to the "on" position.*

        ◊ *Make sure the circuit breaker that controls power to the outlet is turned on.*

        ◊ *Take the television to a repair shop if it is still off.*

5. *Select a channel:*

    - *Choose a program from your local programming guide.*

    - *Push the "up" or "down" arrow on the television to select the program's channel number or push the numbered buttons on the remote control unit that match the program's channel.*

Notice the "alternative" listed as step 3. The worker may or may not have explained this. An observer unfamiliar with the task must always ask: "Is there another way to do this?" to capture this information.

Are you surprised that turning on a television is so complicated? This example highlights small, important steps that can easily be taken for granted or overlooked by an instruction writer.

Once you've completed the guidelines in this chapter, you know *what* to write in your instructions. The remainder of the publication deals with *how* to write your instructions.

4. Replace Jargon

After writing your observation notes, scan them for jargon: specialized words and expressions. Follow these steps to replace words and expressions that are likely to be unfamiliar to your readers:

#	What To Do	How to Do It
1	Make a list of uncommon words and expressions.	• Scan your notes and reference documents. • Highlight uncommon words and phrases, abbreviations, acronyms and words that have a particular meaning when associated with the task you're writing about.
2	Determine whether your readers need to know these words and expressions.	• Readers who will perform this task only once or only casually do not need to learn jargon. Readers who are training to become professionals must learn the jargon of their trade.

#	What To Do	How to Do It
3	Substitute common language for readers who do not need to learn jargon.	• Next to the uncommon terms on your list, write the substitute language. • Use these substitutes in your writing.
4	Introduce the new word or expression to readers who must learn it before you use it in your instructions.	• See Chapter 6 for an explanation about how to introduce new language.

Practice with this example of an instruction for writing an essay:

> *"Write a phenomenological account of an existential moment."*

Which words would you highlight and substitute? Following is an example of a word and phrase replacement list:

Uncommon Terms	Substitutes
phenomenological account	your thoughts & feelings
existential moment	an "aha" incident

Here is the same instruction rewritten in plain language:

"Write your thoughts and feelings about an 'aha' incident you experienced."

No more gobbledygook!

5. Introduce Your Instructions

I read the water heater instructions three times looking for information about changing the temperature. But these instructions were for "Installation," not for ongoing maintenance! If only they'd told me!

Introductions assure readers that:

- They are on the right page
- They are at the beginning
- They will find what they need to complete their task

Follow these three steps when introducing instructions:

1. Determine Whether the Task is Simple or Complex

Simple tasks are straightforward; one step follows another straight to completion. There is no need to stop or put down one part of a project to work on another part. Turning on a television is a simple task.

Complex tasks are performed in different stages; different parts of the project are performed separately and combined later. Assembling a bicycle is a complex task.

23

2. Explain the Purpose of Your Instructions

- Simple Tasks

  - In the first sentence, explain what the instructions will help the reader accomplish.

  - For example:

    "The purpose of these instructions is to teach you how to turn on your television after connecting it to a cable service."

- Complex Tasks

  - Provide an introductory sentence or page that explains the purpose of the instructions.

  - Provide an outline or table of contents listing all the steps.

  - Refer to the page number on which each step is explained.

  - For example:

    These instructions explain how to assemble your Flyer bicycle, Model# 4321. The following list refers to the five steps you must complete.

    1.   Assemble the frame

    2.   Assemble and attach the chain

    3.   Attach the handle bar

    4.   Assemble and attach the pedals

    5.   Assemble and attach the brakes

3. List Instructions by Task Rather than Component

Your readers need to know what to do to get the result they desire. Describe the function of components as you explain the task rather than writing just an explanation of the components. For example:

Write:
1. Turn on the television using the manual controls.
• Locate the Power section
• Locate the TV button – this button turns the TV on.
2. Verify that the television is on.
3. Select a channel.

Rather than writing:
1. TV button
• This button turns the TV on.
2. CBL button
• This button turns the cable box on.
3. Arrow buttons
• These buttons scroll through channels.
4. Numbered buttons
• Press the number of the channel you wish to view.

6. Introduce New Language

Reading an unfamiliar word or phrase while performing an unfamiliar task can ruin a reader's day. If you must introduce new language, explain it before you use it. Follow these five steps to introduce new language:

#	What To Do	Example
1	Tell your readers that you are going to introduce them to a new word, phrase or concept (jargon).	• As a professional, you must become familiar with the concept of "andragogy."

2	Show readers how to pronounce the jargon.	• "Andragogy" is pronounced:
		
		    • *an*-druh-go-gee
		
		    • *an*-druh-go-gee
		
		    • an-druh-go-gee
		
		    • an'-druh-go-gee
		
		    • AN-druh-go-gee
		
		(Each of these is an effective way to show pronunciation. Choose only one way and use it throughout your instructions.)

#	What To Do	Example
3	Define the jargon.	"Andragogy" is the name of a theory that describes ways in which adults learn best. The theory explains that adults choose to learn when they have an immediate or near-future need to know something. Adults benefit from being involved as active participants in the teaching process when they are learning. Relating to their previous knowledge and experience is one way of involving adults in the teaching process. "Andragogy" may also be referred to as 'adult learning' or 'adult learning theory.
4	Relate the jargon to something your readers are already familiar with.	You already know that passive teaching methods used with children, such as lectures and memorization, are boring and sometimes insulting to adults. Andragogy is a more engaging teaching method.

#	What To Do	Example
5	Explain why it is important for your readers to know the jargon.	It is important for you to understand the meaning of "andragogy" because it is the basis of all the learning that will follow. You will see this word often as you train to become an Instructional Technologist.

If you follow the guidelines in this publication, you will be practicing andragogy. But you do not need to know what "andragogy" means to write good instructions.

This is what you must do for general audiences when you write instructions. Give them the principles to follow without expecting them to know jargon and without having them learn new vocabulary that they may never use again.

7. Use Short Sentences and Common Words

Easy-to-read instructions help readers complete their task quickly. A series of short sentences is easier to read than a single sentence containing multiple steps. Single sentences also allow your readers to keep track by checking off steps one sentence at a time. Common words help speed up the reading, too. Follow these four steps:

1. **Write sentences that contain only one complete thought.** Avoid the use of words that connect two or more thoughts such as:

although	and	as
because	but	for (because)
however	nevertheless	nor
now	or	rather
so	that	then
unless	while	yet

Write:	**Rather than writing:**
• Hold the long board with your right hand. • Attach the feet to the end with two holes in it.	• Hold the long board with your right hand <u>as</u> you attach the feet to the end with two holes in it.

29

Write:	Rather than writing:
• Print all your responses on this form. • Use only blue ink. • Sign the bottom.	• Print all your responses on this form in blue ink and sign the bottom.

2. Use 17 words or fewer in each sentence.

- Allow exceptions when you include a short series. For example:

  Put the partitions in the box creating compartments that are large enough for the <u>screws, nails, tacks, washers, and staples</u> that came with the kit

- Allow exceptions when 1, 2 or 3 more words make the sentence clearer.

- Use the "word count" feature in your word processor for help with this step.

3. Substitute uncommon words with familiar or more frequently-used words.

Write:	Rather than writing:
• Use the short screwdriver. • List your footnotes on a separate page at the end of your paper.	• Employ the diminutive utensil. • Append the footnotes to the document.

4. Use shorter rather than longer words (unless the longer word is more familiar).

- Count syllables to determine word length.
- Avoid words of 3 or more syllables if possible.

Write:	Rather than writing:
• Clean the floor. • Stretch the rubber band. • Group the parts by size.	• Sanitize the floor. • Elongate the rubber band. • Categorize the parts by size.

8. Use Abbreviations and Acronyms Carefully

Abbreviations (shortened words) and acronyms (initials) may have more than one meaning or may be unfamiliar to readers. For this reason, they may be misleading or confusing. However, a long word or phrase may be annoying if it is repeated many times. But, if you must choose, it is better to be annoying than misleading and confusing. If you are uncertain about your readers' familiarity with an abbreviation or acronym, spell it out. Follow these steps when you use abbreviations or acronyms:

1. **Answer these four questions to determine if it is appropriate to use an abbreviation or acronym:**

#	Question	Example
1	Are you certain your readers are familiar with the abbreviation or acronym?	The abbreviation "in." for "inches" is familiar to carpenters and others who work with measurements routinely.
2	Are you certain the abbreviation will be more helpful than misleading or confusing?	For carpenters, it would be quicker and more expected to read "in." than "inches."

#	Question	Example
3	Are you sure there are no other words that use the same abbreviation or acronym?	The abbreviation "CD" is quickly recognized as "compact disc" by information technology professionals, and it is quickly recognized as "certificate of deposit" by financial professionals.
4	Are you going to repeat the word or expression more than two times? *After two times, the repetition of a full phrase can become annoying.*	Place the Compact Disc in the "D" drive. Search the Compact Disc for the file. Make the change and save it to the Compact Disc.

If you answered "no" to all four questions, use the complete word or phrase.

If you answered yes to all four questions, continue with steps 2 through 4.

A combination of "yes" and "no" answers means you are uncertain in some areas. Be certain!

2. The first time it appears in your instructions, use the full word or phrase followed by the abbreviation in parentheses.

- Measure 5 <u>inches (in.)</u>.
- Label the compact disc (CD) "Templates."

3. Use the abbreviation or acronym alone in your text after its first appearance.

- Measure five inches (in.). Cut at the 5 <u>in.</u> mark.
- Label the compact disc (CD) "Templates." Put the <u>CD</u> on my desk.

4. Provide a glossary when you use more than two abbreviations and acronyms for unfamiliar words and phrases.

- This applies to manuals and instructions booklets and is not needed in short instructions.

See Chapter 12, *Be Consistent*, Sections 2 and 3 for information about using abbreviations and acronyms consistently.

9. Speak Directly to Your Readers

Hey you! Yes, you! Point your finger at yourself! I'm talking to *you!*

Friendly instructions can make a task seem less challenging. Write instructions that are friendly and easy to follow by "speaking" directly to your readers. Use "you" and "your" in your instructions. Here are a few examples of personalized instructions:

Write:	Rather than writing:
• Hold the long board with <u>your</u> right hand.	• Hold the long board with <u>the</u> right hand.
• The switch is on <u>your</u> right side.	• This switch is on <u>the</u> right side.
• Put <u>your</u> pencil down when <u>you</u> are finished.	• When finished, place <u>the</u> pencil on the desk.
• The next section <u>tells you</u> how write plainly.	• The next section <u>explains</u> how to write plainly.
• Before <u>you</u> begin, make sure <u>you</u> can reach the hammer.	• Before beginning, <u>have the hammer ready</u>.

Speaking directly to your readers can help reduce their nervousness about performing an unfamiliar task.

35

10. Be Positive and Focused

Positive language is encouraging; negative language and distractions can arouse tension, annoyance and anger. Encourage your readers by using positive words in action steps. Avoid negative words and distractions.

1. Avoid these negative words and phrases:

but	can't	cannot	don't
do not	never	no	not

Write:	**Rather than writing:**
• Put the lid on the unit before starting it.	• You <u>can't</u> start the unit unless the lid is on it.
• Choose the answer that satisfies both requirements.	• Answers that <u>don't</u> satisfy both requirements will <u>not</u> be credited.
• If the door remains locked, oil the hinge.	• If you <u>can't</u> open the door, oil the hinge.
• Take the pill after eating food.	• <u>Don't</u> take the pill without first eating some food.
• Avoid the use of negative words and phrases.	• <u>Do not</u> use negative words and phrases.

2. Explain why certain actions must be avoided.

Write:	Rather than writing:
• CAUTION: staples may damage the machine. Remove staples before inserting paper into the machine.	• <u>Don't</u> insert staples into the machine.
• DANGER: You could cause an explosion if you light a match when you smell gas.	• <u>Never</u> light a match when you smell gas.
• Clear the table of all other items to avoid accidentally damaging the unit's finish.	• <u>No </u>other items should be on the table when you put the unit on it.
• Place the paint brush on a flat, out-of-the way, protected surface. This will prevent it from falling and damaging surrounding items.	• Put the paintbrush down, <u>but</u> not on the edge of the can.

3. Avoid expressions that lecture or talk down to readers, such as "you should" and "I want you to..."

Write:	Rather than writing:
• Recall this step from the instructions for Part A.	• <u>You should</u> already be familiar with this step from Part A.
• Pick up the red wire after you have attached the green wire.	• Now <u>I want you to</u> pick up the red wire.

4. Avoid distractions, especially jokes.

- Readers want clear, straightforward guidelines when they read instructions.

- Readers expect the literal meaning of words when they read in instructions, so they may miss the point of a joke.

- Jokes can increase anxiety for someone in the middle of performing an unfamiliar task.

- A sense of humor is a subjective quality; your readers may not share yours.

- Readers are more likely to perceive negative or offensive undertones in jokes that appear in unexpected places such as instructions.

11. Be Exact

The debit machine at the supermarket read: "*Press 'Yes' button if amount is correct.*" I searched and searched for the "Yes" button—while my ice cream melted. There *was no* "*Yes*" button! It meant: "*Press 'Enter' button...*"

Readers expect you to give them all the information they need exactly as they need it. Follow these six steps to write instructions that say exactly what you mean and identify exactly what your readers will see:

1. Provide exact qualities and quantities.

Write:	Rather than writing:
• Give your answer sheet to the instructor.	• Give your answer sheet to <u>her</u>.
• Print the copies on 24-pound, laser-printer-grade white paper that has a brightness rating of 90 or higher.	• Print the copies on <u>white paper</u>.
• Heat the solution until it bubbles.	• <u>Warm</u> the solution.
• Drill the hole with a 1/8-inch drill bit.	• Drill the hole <u>to about the nail size</u>.
• In response to the following question, write an essay of 400 to 600 words, citing three facts with an example of each.	• In response to the following question, <u>write an essay</u>.

Write:	Rather than writing:
• Provide 2 written examples of each problem.	• Provide <u>a few examples</u>.
• From the office, drive west on Main Street for 1.3 miles to the second traffic light, then turn right.	• Go <u>about one mile</u> and turn right at the light.

2. Verify your information:

- An "expert" may tell you the meaning of an acronym or technical term. Verify that meaning using official, documented resources published in the field or discipline of the topic.

- A book, booklet, pamphlet, document or paper may contain information about your topic. Verify that the document is official and accurate. Use original sources, such as academic research reports, whenever possible.

- The people you observe may skip a step and instead, tell you how that step is done. When this happens, perform the step yourself or observe someone else as they actually perform that step to be certain about how it works.

3. State your meaning precisely. For example:

Write:	Rather than writing:
• Move the light switch to the "on" position to illuminate the light.	• Turn the light switch on.

NOTE: A light switch does not get "turned on." Power is already available at the switch. A light switch is a device that is used to illuminate or darken a light.

Write:	Rather than writing:
• Rotate the timer dial clockwise for a full cycle of 360 degrees.	• Rotate the dial for 24 hours.

NOTE: "Rotate the dial for 24 hours" tells readers to spend 24 hours of their time performing the rotation!

4. Use distinctive words and explain words that have multiple meanings:

Write:	Rather than writing:
• Hold the lever down steadily without interruption.	• Hold the lever down constantly. Or • Hold the lever down continually.

NOTE: "Constantly" and "continually" may mean either "steadily without interruption" or "in repeated, interrupted intervals."

5. Avoid prefixes and suffixes that may be unclear, unfamiliar or commonly misused.

Example:	Explanation:
• Semimonthly and bimonthly.	• Semimonthly events occur two times a month and bimonthly events occur once every two months. These are often confused.
• Un-	• Un- may mean "not" as in "unclear" or "to reverse" as in "undo."
• Criteria and criterion	• The "–ia" suffix is plural, meaning many and "-ion" is singular meaning one. Substitute "standards" or standard to avoid confusion.
• Data and datum	• Data is plural, meaning more than one piece of information. Datum means one piece of information. Substitute "information."

6. Substitute exact measurements for general statements.

Write:	Rather than writing::
• Let the material dry for <u>15 minutes</u> before proceeding to the next step.	• Let the material dry for <u>a little while</u> before proceeding to the next step.
• Glue the <u>10-inch</u> bracket to the shelf.	• Glue the <u>long</u> bracket to the shelf.
• Nail the picture hook into the wall <u>4 feet above the center of the fireplace mantle.</u>	• Nail the picture hook into the wall <u>above</u> the fireplace.

See Appendix A for more examples of vague expressions to avoid.

12. Be Consistent

The instructions that came with the new refrigerator read: "*Remove the drip pan from underneath the refrigerator and clean it at least every three months. Wash the tray by hand using mild soap and water.*" Okay, so you're supposed to clean the "drip pan" *and* wash the "tray," right?

Wrong! The drip pan *is* the tray! Different words can mean different things to readers. Refer to the same thing in the same way every time, whether it's an item, a person, place, abbreviation, acronym, numerical expression, or symbol. If there's a standard in your field, use it. If there is no standard, then choose an expression that is visually distinct and least likely to be misread. Eleven situations follow.

1. Names

Choose one name to refer to the same person, place or thing every time in the same instructions. For example:

Use This Name Every Time:	These Alternates Can Cause Confusion:
• Teacher	• Instructor; facilitator; guide; professor; educator; trainer; coach; mentor; tutor.
• Street	• Road; highway; freeway; parkway.
• Car	• Auto; automobile; vehicle; motor vehicle; sedan; coupe.

2. Abbreviations and Symbols

Choose one expression for an abbreviation or symbol and use it every time in the same instructions. For example:

For This Word:	Use Only One of These Abbreviations or Symbols:
• Tablespoon	• T, tbs., or tbsp.
• Feet or foot	• Ft, ft., ft, or '
• Electronic Mail	• E-mail, e-mail, or email
• Post Office Box	• P.O. Box; PO Box; POB; or Box

3. Acronyms

Choose one acronym for an expression and use it every time in the same instructions. For example:

For This Expression:	Use Only One of These Acronyms:
• United States of America	• US; U.S., USA, or U.S.A.
American Association of Retired Persons	• AARP or A.A.R.P.

4. Whole Numbers- Non-financial

Write non-financial whole numbers as either numerals or spelled out words. Whole numbers of two to six digits tend to stand out better when written as numerals. Use a comma before every three-digit group in numerals of four digits or more.

Write:	**Or write:**
• 25	• Twenty-five
• 140	• One hundred forty
• 1,500	• One thousand five hundred
• 15,355	• Fifteen thousand three hundred and fifty-five
• 100,000	• One hundred thousand
• 2,000,000	• Two million

5. Whole Numbers Less Than 10

Write whole numbers less than 10 (1 through 9) as either numerals or spelled out words. Although the rules of grammar suggest spelling-out these numbers, numerals are clearer and quicker to read in instructions. However, when a number is used as the first word of a sentence, spell it out. For example:

Write:	Rather than writing:
• Tap the key 2 times.	• Tap the key two times.
• Pick 7 cards.	• Pick seven cards.

Note: In an instruction action step, use only a verb as the first word of a sentence to avoid concerns about the use of numbers—see Chapter 18: Begin Action Steps with "Do" and "Degree" Words for more information.

6. Whole Numbers of 7 Digits or More

Either spell out *or* use numerals to represent values of millions, billions and greater. Use the same expression consistently. For example:

Write:	Or write:
• 12,000,000	• 12 million or twelve million.

7. Zero

Choose one expression for the numerical value of zero and use it consistently.

- Use either the spelled-out word "zero" or the numeral "0."

8. Fractions

Either spell-out fraction values or use numerals. Numerals tend to be easier and quicker to read in instructions. Choose one and use it consistently.

Write:	Or write:
• one quarter	• 1/4

Note: If you are using a computer and your software allows you to express fraction characters (¼ versus 1/4), use this feature consistently or not at all.

9. Whole Numbers with Fractions

Write numerals for the combination of whole numbers and fractions. Use the ampersand or "and" sign (&) to show the relationship between the two. For example:

Write:	Rather than writing:
• 5 & 1/4	• 5 1/4, 5-1/4 or 5 and 1/4

10. Decimal Fractions

Use a zero before the decimal to highlight it and make the fraction value clearer to your readers.

Write:	Rather than writing:
• 0.125	• .125
• 0.5	• .5

11. Quantity and Measurement Statements

Statements that include both numerals and measurement statements must also be used consistently.

Write:	Or write:
• Increase the amount by <u>6 percent</u>. • Make a pencil mark at <u>4 inches</u>.	• Increase the amount by <u>6%</u>. • Make a pencil mark at <u>4"</u>.

Use a hyphen between a numeral and a word when the quantity is used to describe a feature of something. For example:

Write:	Rather than writing:
• Earn a <u>6-percent</u> interest rate. • Cut <u>4-inch</u> lengths.	• Earn a <u>6 percent</u> interest rate. • Cut <u>4 inch</u> lengths.

Combined quantity and measurement statements are clearer when the quantity is spelled out and a numeral is used for the measurement that follows it. For example:

Write:	**Rather than writing:**
• Buy twelve 4-inch hooks.	• Buy 12 4-inch hooks. • Buy twelve four-inch hooks. • Buy 12 4" hooks.

12. Financial Values

For dollars-and-cents statements, use the decimal expression every time when there are "cents" amounts in any one expression. For example:

Write:	**Rather than writing:**
• Pay the $100.<u>00</u> fee and save $59.<u>95</u>.	• Pay the $<u>100</u> fee and save $<u>59.95</u>.

NOTE: Readers may wonder whether an amount has been forgotten when the decimal places appear only some of the time.

13. Be Easy on the Eyes

Cluttered or crowded text is distracting; it requires readers to concentrate more on reading than on completing their task. Text that stands out helps readers capture the information they need quickly. It also helps them keep track of the step they're working on. The 12 steps in this chapter can help you write your instructions in reader-friendly formats.

1. Set Wide Side Margins

Create side margins using at least 35% of the horizontal space on your page or screen. This example demonstrates how to calculate these margins:

Instruction for an 8.5-inch wide page:	Calculation:
• Multiply 8.5 inches by 35 %.	• 8.5 x 0.35 = 2.975 inches
• Round your answer up to the nearest "0" decimal place.	• 2.975 = 3.0 inches
• Divide your answer by two (one for each side margin).	• 3.0/2.0 = 1.5 inches
• Set the left and right margins at 1.5 inches each.	• Use the ruler on your word processor or a manual ruler.

2. Set Large Top and Bottom Margins

Create top and bottom margins that use at least 25% of the vertical space. This example demonstrates how to calculate these margins:

Instruction for an 11-inch long page:	Calculation:
• Multiply 11 inches by 25 %.	• 11 x 0.25 = 2.75 inches
• Round your answer up to the nearest "0" decimal place.	• 2.75 = 3.0 inches
• Divide your answer by two (one for each margin).	• 3.0/2.0 = 1.5 inches
• Set the top and bottom margins at 1.5 inches each.	• Use the ruler on your word processor or a manual ruler.

3. Present Steps on the Same Page

Adjust your margins to allow a complete step to fit on one page or screen.

- Break large steps down into smaller steps if necessary.

- For single-page instructions, center the complete block of text horizontally and vertically by increasing the margin spacing (see steps 1 and 2).

- For manuals and booklets, start at the same place near the top of each page and leave more white space at the bottom.

4. Indent Paragraphs

Indent paragraphs five spaces, just like this one and the one that follows.

This is the second paragraph in this section. Notice how the indentation makes the text stand out as a new idea.

5. Separate Paragraphs

Leave more space between paragraphs than between sentences within paragraphs. This provides a separation that makes text easier to read.

Notice that the space above this sentence is greater than the space between the two lines of this sentence.

6. List Items

Use vertical lists rather than words separated by commas when the listed items must be carefully noticed.

Write:	**Rather than writing:**
Choose one of the primary colors: - red - yellow - blue	Choose one of the primary colors: red, yellow, blue.

7. Separate Listed Items

Leave extra space between items in lists. For example:

Write:	**Rather than writing:**
- red - yellow - blue	- red - yellow - blue

8. Center Short Text

When sentences can be completed on one line, center the text. For example:

Write:
1. Red is the first color of the spectrum. 2. Yellow is in the middle of the spectrum. 3. Blue is near the end of the spectrum.

Rather than writing:
1. Red is the first color of the spectrum. 2. Yellow is in the middle of the spectrum. 3. Blue is near the end of the spectrum.

9. Indent Subordinate Steps

Indent activities that are part of a step or that provide more information about how to perform the step.

Step 1. Stir the paint.
      • Use a clean, wooden stick.
      • Stir slowly to avoid splashing.
Step 2. Dip the brush bristles halfway into the paint.
      • Wipe the brush on the can's edge.

10. Use Easy-to-Read Fonts

Use a serif font. A serif font has lines that finish off the main strokes of a letter, like the end caps on this letter: T. Serif fonts put more space between letters making them easier to read.

Serif Fonts	Sans (without) Serif Fonts:
• Times New Roman • Courier New	• Arial • Franklin Gothic Book

11. Select An Easy-to-Read Print Size

Use 12-point or 10-point print. Print larger than 12-point type is good for emphasis but is tiring to read. Print smaller than 10-point type is difficult to read at a glance.

Select:	Save for special effects:
• 12-point type size • 10-point type size	• 14-point type size • 20-point type

12. Emphasize Key Words

Key words are elements of instructions that are critical for readers to follow. Emphasis helps readers see key words at a glance and makes it difficult to overlook them. Following are seven methods for emphasizing words or phrases:

Method:	Example:
1. Capitalize	First attach the RED wire.
2. Highlight or bold	Reach in and **pull** the lever.
3. Increase Type Size	Stop winding when the line is tense.
4. Underline	Insert paper <u>face down</u>.
5. Italicize	Push the *red lever*.
6. Colorize when your medium allows.	Push the red lever. (The word "red" would be printed in the color red in the above sentence.)
7. Combine two or more of these emphasizing methods.	• Combine **bold and underline.** • Combine *CAPITALS* and *ITALICS*.

14. Identify Necessary Resources

Few things are more frustrating than lacking the necessary time, equipment, tools, documents and manuals to perform a task. Tell you readers what resources they will need before they begin the task.

Resource:	Examples:
1. Time	The time average you calculated during your observations.
2. Equipment	Floor mat; ladder; safety glasses; calculator;
3. Hand tools	Pencil; pen; paper; hammer; pliers; screwdriver (type and size); measuring tape; gloves;
4. Documents	Licenses; certificates; identification.
5. Manuals	Dictionary; thesaurus; encyclopedia; text book; owners manual

Example:

Allow 10 minutes to change the bulb. Have available:

- *a stepladder*
- work gloves
- a tray to hold the old and new gloves

15. Inform Readers of Hazards

Help your readers stay safe by warning them about potentially dangerous situations before they begin the task. Follow these three steps:

1. Place an Obvious Hazard Notice in Your Text

- Place a hazard notice where readers will be certain to see it. Use words like:

    Caution

    Danger

    Warning

- Exaggerate the appearance of the hazard notice by emphasizing it as a key word or phrase. (See Chapter 13: *Be Easy on the Eyes;* Section 12, *Emphasize Key Words, page 55.*) For example:

    CAUTION!

    DANGER!

    WARNING!

2. Explain How to Avoid the Hazard

Provide clear instructions for avoiding the hazard rather than assuming it will be obvious to your reader. Examples:

- Be sure the light switch is in the "off" position before you change the light bulb.

- Make sure the ladder does not wobble. Check that all four feet of the ladder are securely placed on the floor.

3. Explain the Potential Danger

Emphasize the importance of your readers' safety by giving them a reason to take precautions. Examples:

- This will help you avoid electrical shock.

This will help you to avoid falling off the ladder and injuring yourself.

16. Arrange Steps in Order

Outline the steps before you write. An outline:

- Helps you sort information into a sequence;
- Helps you verify that all steps are included;
- Enables you to guide your readers through an uninterrupted sequence;
- Prevents you from having to backtrack.

Use this definition to determine which actions you may group together as a single step:

> A <u>step</u> is part of a task that can be performed without a break or pause. A step may include several actions. When a step is complete, the task can be continued from that point without having to backtrack.

If you numbered the steps in your notes during your observations (see Chapter 3: *Observe a Worker and Take Notes*) then outlining will be easy. Follow these four steps to arrange *your* steps in order before you write instructions:

1. Sort Your Observation Notes

Sort your observation notes into groups of steps in the order in which they must be performed.

- When a single step involves more than one activity, give the step one name and number, and indent and list the related, or subordinate, actions below it (just like the one you are reading now).

- You may have numbered subordinate actions in your observation notes. If so, renumber your steps during this outlining process.

2. Group Steps into Phases for Complex Tasks

For complex tasks that require manuals or booklets (see Chapter 5: *Introduce Your Instructions*), group your steps into phases. A phase is a group of steps that complete part of a task which may be set aside while other parts are worked on, such as the components of a bicycle frame or a book. Phases may be separated into chapters in your instructions, as they are in this publication.

3. Note Options and Choices

When your readers must choose between one step and another:

- Make a note for your readers to skip one or the other step.

- Use the same number for alternative steps and distinguish them with letters, such as 1A and 1B.

4. Present Information in Its Order of Appearance

Always present information in the order in which your reader will see it. For example:

Write:	Rather than writing:
• Click on "Tools," then click on "Options."	• Click on "Options" on the "Tools" menu.

5. Follow Your Outline While Writing Instructions

Once you've organized your notes into a sequential outline, follow it as you write your instructions. Refer to it often to keep you on track and prevent the need for rework.

17. Include Checkpoints at Critical Stages

In many tasks, there is a point at which the next step depends on the successful completion of an earlier step. Remind your readers to verify that they have completed the earlier step successfully. This is a "checkpoint."

Checkpoints are different from hazard notices (see Chapter 15: *Inform Readers of Hazards)*. Hazard notices inform readers of potential dangers that exist regardless of their actions or inaction. Checkpoints remind readers about earlier steps they must have completed to avoid difficulties. They help readers avoid dangerous situations that *they* may create through their actions or inaction. No matter how clearly you write your instructions, readers may skip steps. Including checkpoints in instructions emphasizes the importance of successfully completing earlier steps.

Follow the four steps in this chapter to write checkpoints into your instructions. Examples are provided at the end of the chapter.

1. Begin Checkpoints with Timing Statements

Tell readers they must take action *now*. Use opening statements such as:

- At this point…
- Before you continue…
- Now…

2. Include Prompts

Include cue phrases that prompt readers to verify that an earlier step has been successfully completed. Here are a few examples of cue phrases:

- …be certain…
- …be sure…
- …check…
- …confirm…
- …ensure…
- …make sure…
- …verify…

3. Describe the Earlier Step

Restate the earlier step that is critical to completion of the current step.

4. Explain the Reason

Describe the consequences that may result from lack of performance of the earlier step.

Checkpoint Examples
Example 1:
At this point (1) *be certain* (2) *all four feet of the ladder are flat on the floor* (3). *This prevents the ladder from wobbling and causing you to fall* (4).

Example 2:

Now (1) *verify* (2) *that you have entered your social security number without dashes* (3). *This prevents your information from being deleted* (4).

18. Begin Action Steps with "Do" and "Degree" Words

Get right to the point when your readers must take action. Tell them what to do and how forcefully or intensely to do it. The four steps in this chapter explain how to write action steps in your instructions.

1. Begin with an Action Word

Start each action-step instruction with a word that tells your readers exactly what action to take: a "do" word. Here are a few examples:

- <u>Click</u> on the words that most closely match your opinion.

- <u>Turn</u> the dial clockwise.

- <u>Print</u> your first name.

- <u>Plug</u> the cord into the back of the unit.

- <u>Steer</u> to the right.

2. Use Two "Do" Words for Coordinated Actions

Use two "do" words only when you reader must do two things at the same time. For example:

- <u>Hold</u> the "Ctrl" key down while you <u>click</u> on words that most closely match your opinion.

- <u>Push</u> the dial in as you <u>turn</u> it clockwise.

- <u>Press</u> as you <u>print</u> your name.

- <u>Hold</u> the cover open as you <u>plug</u> the cord into the unit.

67

- <u>Brake</u> and <u>steer</u> at the same time.

3. Describe the Force or Intensity

Use a "degree" word to describe the intensity, speed, or strength with which your reader must perform the action. For example:

- Hold the "Ctrl" key down <u>firmly</u> while you click on words that most closely match your opinion.

- Push the dial in <u>forcefully</u> as you turn it clockwise.

- Press <u>hard</u> as you print your name.

- Hold the cover open <u>wide</u> as you plug the cord into the unit.

- Brake <u>gently</u> and steer at the same time.

4. Separate Actions

Write each action on a separate line. For example:

- <u>Locate</u> the list labeled "Opinions" on your computer screen.

- <u>Move</u> your cursor to the column in which the list appears.

- <u>Hold</u> the "Ctrl" key down firmly as you <u>click</u> on the words that best describe your opinion.

- <u>Release</u> the "Ctrl" key after clicking on your word choices.

- <u>Press</u> the "Enter" key.

Compare the Effect of Do-Word Instructions	
Clear Instruction:	**Less Clear:**
<u>Hold</u> the "Ctrl" key down firmly while you click on words that most closely describe your opinion.	Your opinion may not be stated exactly in the list, so click on words that are closest to it.
<u>Push</u> in forcefully as you turn the dial clockwise.	The dial is designed to be turned in a clockwise direction.
<u>Press</u> hard as you print your name.	When printing your name, be sure to press hard.
<u>Hold</u> the cover open wide as you plug the cord into the outlet in the back of the unit.	There is a covered outlet in the back of the unit where the plug goes.
<u>Brake gently and steer</u> at the same time.	You must move your vehicle to the right, so steer in that direction with the brakes on.

See Appendix B more examples of "Do" words.

19. Describe People, Locations and Things with "Picture" Words

The instructions said: "*Now push the button on your remote control unit.*" Yikes! There are twenty buttons on the unit. Some are round, some are square, some are triangular, and some are crescent-shaped. Which one am I supposed to push?

Use "picture" words to help your readers identify things and people. Picture words describe exactly what your readers will see. Picture words help create a visual image by:

- naming people, places and things, and
- naming features and characteristics of specific people, places and things.

The four steps in this chapter explain how to identify people, places and things in your instructions.

1. Identify People, Places and Things

Use a word that identifies the person, place or thing your readers must recognize. For example:

- Tell the <u>man</u>.
- Push the <u>button</u>.
- Turn onto the <u>driveway</u>.
- Pick up the <u>wrench</u>.

Now add more information. Continue to Step 2.

2. Describe Features or Characteristics

Add a word or phrase that describes the features or characteristics of the person, place or thing your readers must recognize. For example:

- Tell the <u>tall</u> man.

- Push the <u>triangular-shaped yellow</u> button.

- Turn onto the <u>grey gravel</u> driveway.

- Pick up the <u>3/4-inch crescent</u> wrench.

3. Describe the Location

Use words that tell your readers where to find the person, place or thing they must recognize. For example:

- Tell the tall man who is <u>standing near the door</u>.

- Push the triangular-shaped yellow button <u>located in the center of the remote control unit</u>.

- Turn onto the grey gravel driveway <u>on the right-hand side of the street</u>.

- Pick up the 3/4-inch crescent wrench <u>in the blue plastic bag</u>.

71

4. Avoid Pronouns

Avoid the use of the following words when referring to a person, place or thing to prevent confusion:

he	her	him	his
it	she	them	their
this	that	these	those

Compare the Effect of Picture Words	
Picture-word Instruction:	**Vague Instruction:**
Tell the tall man who is standing near the door.	• Tell him.
Push the triangular-shaped, yellow button located in the center of the remote-control unit.	• Push it. • Push the button.
Turn onto the grey gravel driveway on the right-hand side of the street.	• Turn onto it. • Turn onto the driveway. • Turn there.
Pick up the ¾-inch crescent wrench from the blue plastic bag.	• Pick it up. • Pick up the wrench.

See Appendix C for more examples of "Picture" words.

20. Describe Noises with "Sound" Words

The first time I heard the new automatic ice-maker fill its tray, I almost jumped out of my shoes. It sounded like a helicopter trying to take off: whir, whir, whir; wheep, wheep, wheep; groan, groan, groan. I panicked thinking I must have installed the water line incorrectly. It took a half hour to retrace my steps, only to discover that everything was okay. The ice-maker was supposed to make those noises!

Tell your readers what noises to expect when things are working well. Also tell them what noises may be a sign of trouble and what to do about it. The two steps in this chapter explain how to identify noises in your instructions.

1. Find "Sound" Words

Choose or invent a word or words that imitate the noises your reader may hear. For example:

- The ice-maker makes noises that sound like <u>whir</u>, <u>wheep</u> and <u>groan</u> when working properly. <u>Swooshes</u> could be a sign of trouble.

- Turn the gas cap clockwise until you hear three <u>clicks</u>. No sound at all could be a sign of trouble. Unscrew the cap and try again...

- The fax machine makes a <u>grinding</u> noise while it is printing.

- The paper shredder makes a <u>growling</u> noise when working properly.

73

2. Describe the Intensity

Add a word or phrase that describes the volume, intensity or other characteristic of a noise. For example:

- The ice-maker makes <u>high-pitched, shrill</u> noises that sound like whir, wheep and groan when working properly.

- Turn the gas cap clockwise until you hear three <u>loud</u> clicks.

- The fax machine makes a <u>rough</u> grinding noise while it is printing.

- The paper shredder makes a <u>gritty</u> growling noise when working properly.

See Appendix D for more examples of "Sound" words.

21. Describe Flavors with "Taste" Words

When my home-made barbeque sauce didn't taste like barbeque sauce, I backtracked to be sure I'd included all the ingredients. They were all there. The sauce tasted fine after it was heated.

If you are writing instructions or recipes for things that have distinct flavors, describe the tastes your readers can expect at different phases of the task. This will help them continue with certainty and without interruption. The two steps in this chapter explain how to identify tastes in your instructions.

1. Find "Taste" Words

Choose a word that identifies the taste your readers can expect at each phase. For example:

- The sauce will taste <u>bitter </u>before it is heated.

- The sauce will taste <u>sweet</u> after it is heated.

- If the sauce tastes <u>bitter,</u> add ¼ teaspoon of salt.

2. Describe Similarities

Refer to something similar to the taste your readers can expect when there is no exact word to describe it. For example:

- The sauce will taste <u>like vinegar</u> before it is heated.

- The sauce will taste <u>vinegary</u> before it is heated.

See Appendix E, Section 1, for more examples of "Taste" words.

22. Describe Textures with "Touch" Words

The wallpaper adhesive was lumpy when I opened the can. I thought I'd gotten a bad batch, so I returned it. The sales clerk asked me if I had stirred it. Lumpiness was normal; stirring made the mixture smooth.

If you are writing instructions for things that have texture, describe the consistency or feel your readers can expect at different phases of the task. This will ensure them that things are going well. The two steps in this chapter explain how to identify textures in your instructions.

1. Find "Touch" Words

Choose a word that identifies the texture your readers can expect at each phase. For example:

- The adhesive is <u>lumpy</u> when you first open the can.

- Keep stirring until the adhesive is <u>smooth</u>.

- If the wood still feels <u>rough</u> continue sanding with fine-grade sandpaper.

2. Describe Similarities

Refer to something similar to the texture your readers can expect when there is no exact word to describe it. For example:

- If the wood feels <u>like wool</u>, continue sanding.

- The wood feels <u>scratchy</u> after the first sanding.

See Appendix E, Section 2, for more examples of "Touch" words.

76

23. Describe Odors with "Smell" Words

The glue smelled rancid, so I threw it away and bought a new tube. It smelled the same, so I took it back and exchanged it. I tested another new tube in the store. It smelled bad, too. The sales clerk explained that after a few minutes of exposure to the air, the smell goes away.

If you are writing instructions for things that have an odor, describe the smell your readers can expect at different phases of the task. This will help them complete their task quickly and correctly. The two steps in this chapter explain how to identify odors in your instructions.

1. Find "Smell" Words

Choose a word that identifies the odor or aroma your readers can expect at each phase of their task. For example:

- The glue smells <u>rancid</u> when you first open the tube.

- After a few minutes, the glue becomes <u>odorless</u>.

2. Describe similarities

Refer to something similar to the odor your readers can expect when there is no exact word to describe it. For example:

- It is normal for the glue to smell <u>like gasoline</u> when you first open the tube.

- Throw the glue away if it smells <u>like rotten eggs</u>.

See Appendix E, Section 3, for more examples of "Smell" words.

24. Illustrate Your Instructions

You know the old adage: a picture is worth a thousand words. But the wrong kind of picture is worth a thousand cuss words! Determine the appropriate type of illustration to use in your instructions. Start by identifying the activity your readers must perform:

1. Assemble, control, manipulate or operate an object.

2. Choose between two situations with each having two categories.

3. Select multiple options.

4. Make decisions at intermediate steps.

5. Mentally organize or compare information.

6. Physically arrange information.

7. Calculate answers.

Using the chart on the next page, determine the type of illustration that is best suited to your readers' activity. Follow these steps to read the chart:

- Look in the left-hand column for the type of activity your readers must perform.

- Scan across the activity line until you find a number.

- Look at the top of the column in which the number appears.

- The column title in which the number appears identifies the type of illustration to use.

- The number refers to the section in this chapter that explains how to use the chart.

Select an Appropriate Illustration						
Illustration ➜ **Activity** ⬇	Photograph or Drawing(s)	Four-Box Chart (Quadrant)	Combination Table (Matrix)	Flow Chart	Graph	Worksheet
1. Handle an object	**1**					
2. Choose one of two options		**2**				
3. Select multiple options			**3**			
4. Make decisions				**4**		
5. Organize thoughts					**5**	
6. Arrange information						**6**
7. Calculate answers						**6**

Once you have selected a type of illustration, note the number in its column. For an explanation of how to use the illustration, go to that numbered section in this chapter.

1. Photographs and Drawings

Photographs and drawings (or diagrams) help readers to quickly identify parts, characteristics and features of people, places and things.

1a. Photographs

If possible, use a photograph show an exact image of that which your readers will see. When you make a photograph:

- Use color contrast so that details stand out clearly

- Include other items in the picture to demonstrate the relative size of the object of your readers' attention.

1b. Drawings and Diagrams

Use a drawing when your readers must assemble, control, manipulate or operate an object, and a photograph is not available, not possible or not affordable within your budget. Following is an example of labeling outside an item:

Diagram of shapes:

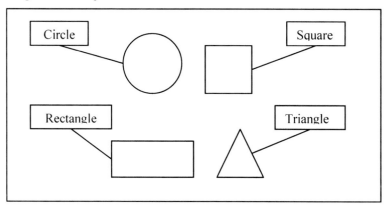

When you include a drawing or diagram:

- Place it on the same page or the page facing the text that explains it whenever possible.

- Label the view: top, bottom, side, angled or other positions

- Use pointers when you must place labels outside the image.

- Include dimensions when applicable or necessary.

- Show features in proper proportion to each other

1c. Sequential Drawings

Use sequential drawings to show your readers what their project must look like at different stages. Sequential drawings help readers measure their progress and avoid backtracking. Here is an example:

Sequential drawings illustrating the construction of a square:

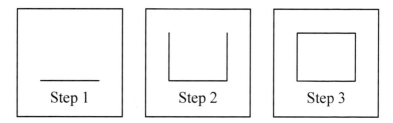

When you create a sequential drawing:

- Follow the guidelines for drawings in Step1b.

- Arrange the drawings left-to-right or top-to-bottom, in order of completion.

- Show the step number in each separate drawing.

2. Four-Box or Quadrant Charts

Use a four-box or quadrant chart when your readers must choose between two situations, each having two categories. These charts help readers quickly locate the instruction they need. Consider this example:

Determine How to Treat a Faucet in a Home-Remodeling Project		
Situation → **Category ↓**	**Faucet Leaks**	**Faucet Does Not Leak**
Hardware is New	**1.** Repair the faucet now	**2.** Keep the faucet
Hardware is Old	**3.** Replace the faucet now	**4.** Replace the faucet later

The instruction at the intersection of "Faucet Does Not Leak" and "Hardware is Old" (#4) tells the reader to replace the faucet later. When creating a quadrant chart:

- Give it a title that describes the step.

- Pair like features together in the top line and the left-hand column.

- Number each of the four boxes left-to-right, and top-to-bottom.

- Explain how to read the chart.

- Put an instruction in each box.

3. Combination or Matrix Tables

Use a combination or matrix table when your reader must select from many combinations of options, or would be helped by seeing many features at a glance. Write your message at the intersection of two conditions, just as in a four-box/quadrant chart. A combination/matrix table was used on page 75. Here is another example:

Determine the Color of Hats Available by Size			
Size → Color ↓	Small	Medium	Large
Red	Yes	Yes	No
Yellow	Yes	No	Yes
Blue	No	Yes	Yes

Is a medium-sized hat available in yellow? Follow the "Medium" column down to the intersection of the "Yellow" line to find the answer ("No").

When you create a combination/matrix table:

- Give it a title that describes the step.
- Explain how to read the table.
- Make sure you have an equal number of conditions for rows and columns.
- Fit the table onto one page or screen.
- Use one word or a symbol at the intersections.
- Use footnotes to refer to additional comments.

4. Flowcharts

Use a flowchart when your readers must make decisions at intermediate steps. Flowcharts are maps of the steps and decision points in a process. Using arrows, lines and brief instructions, flowcharts help readers to "see" the order of a procedure. Here is an example:

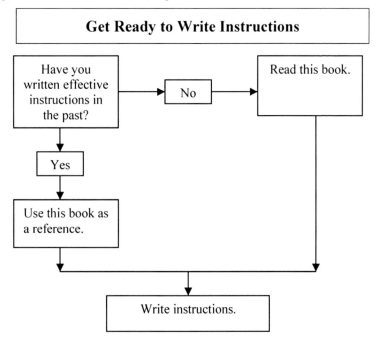

Get Ready to Write Instructions

| Have you written effective instructions in the past? | No | Read this book. |

Yes

Use this book as a reference.

Write instructions.

When you include a flowchart:

- Give it a title that describes the step, phase or task explained in the flowchart.

- Use the same title on each page when the flowchart requires more than page.

- Number the pages in the title box as 1-of-#, 2-of-#, etc. when more than one page is required.

5. Graphs and Charts

Use a graph or chart when your readers must mentally organize or compare information without the need to write or calculate. Graphs and charts show relationships between topics and help readers to quickly compare concepts, trends or results. Many types of charts and graphs can show the same information. Only two examples are shown in this chapter.

Bar-chart example:

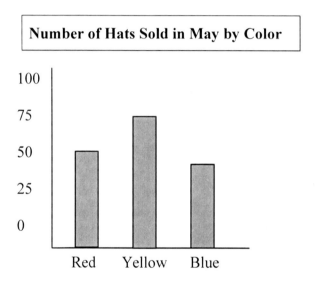

Number of Hats Sold in May by Color

How many yellow hats were sold in May? Find the color along the line at the bottom of the graph. Follow its bar to the top end. Look to the left from the top of the bar and find the number. Approximately 75 hats were sold in May.

Line-graph example:

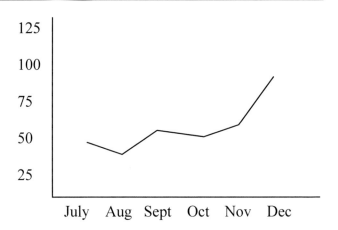

Number of Hats Sold July through December

How many hats were sold in October? Find the month along the line at the bottom of the graph. Look up from the month to the point on the lines. Look to the left for the quantity. Approximately 60 hats were sold in October.

During which month were hat sales lowest? Find the lowest point along the lines in the graph. Look below it to find the corresponding month. Sales were lowest in August.

When you create a graph or chart:

- Give it a title describing the information it contains.

- Explain how to read the graph or chart.

- Fit it and its explanation onto the same page.

- Make increments as specific as the reader needs.

- Use as few words as possible.

6. Worksheets

Use a worksheet when your readers must physically arrange information or calculate answers. Worksheets are structured forms that contain space and instructions for entering answers. They help readers organize their work and minimize the chance that they might miss steps.

You have already used a worksheet in Chapter 1: *Allow Enough Time* on page 2. Examples of completed worksheets are shown on pages 8 and 9.

When you create a worksheet:

- Give the worksheet a title that explains its purpose.

- Separate the worksheet from your instructions or make it easy to reproduce.

- Include a separate line for every step.

- Number every line in the order of the steps.

- Give each line the number matching text that explains the step in detail (see pages 3 through 7).

- Tell readers exactly what to do on each line and in the text that has the same number.

- Keep in one column numbers that are to be added.

- Create separate, highlighted boxes for totals.

- Block out unused spaces.

- Create spaces large enough for manual entries.

- Provide a completed example.

A Note about Illustrations in this Chapter:

The purpose of this publication is to explain how to *write* the text of your instructions. This "Illustrations" chapter is included to encourage you to supplement your text with illustrations and to explain how to *choose* an appropriate type of illustration for your readers.

Creating illustrations is a related but separate topic. Information about how to create illustrations is explained in detail in many other books and on web sites. Search a library or the Internet for more information about illustrations that interest you, other types of illustrations that are available, and the rules for using specific types of illustrations.

Also check your software applications. Many spreadsheet and word processing programs have a chart-making feature that produces charts and graphs from your data.

25. Guide Readers in Solving Problems

Sometimes things go wrong. Your readers rely on you to research what can go wrong and tell them about common problems, solutions and contacts. When you know what might go wrong, tell your readers what to do about it. For problems you're unable to anticipate, tell them where they can get help.

1. Encourage Your Readers

In the first sentence in which you introduce a potential problem, assure your readers that it is more likely to be caused by technical issues than human error. Put their minds at ease so they can resolve the problem calmly without becoming frustrated. For example, say:

- *"If the unit is plugged in and the green light still does not come on, there may be a problem with the unit."*

- *"If you get a different result than the one on the answer sheet, you may have an incorrect answer sheet."*

2. Offer Possible Technical Causes

Follow your encouragement with an explanation of what may be causing the problem. Continuing the previous examples:

- *"The bulb may be burned out or the wiring may be defective."*

- *"There are two versions of the answer sheet."*

91

3. Explain Problems that May Occur in Simple Tasks

Explain how to determine the cause of common problems in simple tasks. Continuing with the previous examples, say:

- *"Open the back door and remove the bulb from the center of the unit. Replace it with the spare."*

- *"Get a current answer sheet from the letter tray on the desk in the front of the room."*

4. Provide a Problem-Solving Guide for Complex Tasks

For tasks with many steps, provide a "problem-solving" or "trouble-shooting" guide. List all the problems you can anticipate and their solutions in a separate area of your instructions.

Use a combination or matrix table (see Chapter 24: *Illustrate Your Instructions*; Section 3, page 79) to organize this information so your readers may scan it quickly.

5. Provide Contact Information

Tell you readers where they can get help. Be specific to prevent them from doing the wrong thing:

- *"Between the hours of 8AM and 5PM EST Monday through Friday, call the Customer Support Center at 1-800-555-8888. During other hours, page the on-duty technician at 1-800-555-9999."*

"Ask your exam proctor for a current answer sheet if none are on the desk."

26. Refer to Additional Information

The people who sold me a sewing machine knew a lot about introducing new information. First, they showed me how to do just the basics (that's all I wanted to know—I'm no seamstress!) Then they offered me a free seat in a class four weeks later. By the time I got to the class, the nervous heebie-jeebies of working with the new machine had gone away. I was ready to learn a few advanced techniques without feeling overwhelmed by a lack of familiarity with the machine. And I was ready to buy accessories to help me perform those advanced techniques—very smart of them!

After your readers successfully accomplish the basic task, they may become ready and interested in advancing their knowledge and skills. Separate advanced instructions and references from basic instructions. Follow these four steps to offer additional information in your instructions:

1. Describe Advanced Features and Operations

Acknowledge your readers' accomplishment and offer them enhanced use or knowledge. For example:

- *"Now that you have mastered the basic operations of your cooling unit, you may be interested in using it outdoors."*

- *"Now that you have learned these calculations, you may be eligible to take the advanced placement test."*

93

2. Describe Requirements

Tell your readers what they must have or know to advance their use or knowledge. Continuing the previous examples:

- *"You must have an overhead shelter to operate the unit outdoors."*

- *"You must already have a license to take the advanced placement test."*

3. Reference Advanced Instructions

Tell your readers where they may locate advanced information or instructions. Continuing the examples:

- *The instructions for outdoor use are on page 119 and on our website at http://www.coolingexample.com."*

- *"Call 1-800-555-2222 to receive an application by mail for the advanced placement test.*

4. Refer to Independent Learning Resources

Describe references your readers may obtain to learn more about the subject on their own. Give specific advice for locating these resources, which may include:

- Books
- Magazines
- Web Sites
- Professional Organizations
- Educational Institution

27. Describe "The End"

I carefully followed the instructions for setting up my fax machine: assemble the parts; insert the ink cartridge; plug in the cords; roll over the phone lines…huh? What does *that* mean? I finally found an explanation but it didn't have anything to do with my situation. So I kept on reading more things that didn't matter to me. Eventually I thought I'd just give it a try. It worked! I was finished but didn't know it!

Follow these three steps to tell your readers when they have reached the last step of the task:

1. Tell Readers When They Are Finished

Tell your readers when they have reached the last step of their task. For example:

- *"You have completed the last step."*

- *"You have completed this assignment."*

- *"If you have only one phone line, you are now finished."*

2. Describe Success

Explain what your readers will see or be able to do when they have successfully completed the task. For example:

- *"A green light will appear when you push the 'on' button if there are no problems."*

- *"An alarm will sound when you plug in the unit if it is set up correctly."*

- *"You will be able to send fax messages if the connections are correct."*

3. Explain What to Do If Unsuccessful

Tell your readers what to do if their result is unsuccessful at the completion of the last step. Follow the steps listed in Chapter 25: *Guide Readers in Solving Problems.*

4. Congratulate Your Readers

Acknowledge your readers' success and launch them into enjoying their achievement. For example:

- *"Congratulations on having successfully assembled your unit! Enjoy it!"*

- *"Congratulations on your excellent set-up! Enjoy the peace of mind in knowing you are protected!"*

  "Congratulations on calculating the correct answer! You are well prepared to begin the next phase of your program!"

28. Test Your Instructions

The technician read from his instruction manual as he guided me: *"Click on 'File' and a drop-down menu will appear. On the drop-down menu, click 'New Identities.'"* Oops! There was no "New Identities" label! If those instructions had been tested, we would have had a much shorter and happier conversation!

When you think you've finished writing your instructions, you're at a new beginning. There's still a lot of work to do! This chapter explains how to test your instructions.

1. Create a Worksheet

Do you remember the observations described in Chapter 3? You need to observe again, but this time you must choose workers who are *un*familiar with the task and ask them to follow your instructions. Before you arrange these observations, create a worksheet for notes. Include blank spaces for each step and its activities. Make the space large enough for at least two hand-written sentences. Number each space the same as you've numbered your instructions, for example:

Instruction-Test Worksheet
Observation Notes
Step 1:
• Step 1-1:
• Step 1-2:
Step 2:
• Step 2-1:
Step 3:
• Step 3-1:
• Step 3-2:
• Step 3-3:

2. Observe an Unskilled Worker

Follow these steps for conducting test observations.
You will be testing *your instructions*—not the workers!

	Steps for Observing	
#	**What To Do**	**How To Do It**
1	Ask for volunteers.	Make separate appointments to meet with them individually.
2	Observe separately.	Keep workers separate in time and/or location so they don't try to "help" each other.
3	Give workers a draft copy of your instructions.	Make sure they understand that you are testing the instructions and not their performance.
4	Give workers a copy of your worksheet for notes.	Ask workers to write questions or concerns they may have for each step.
5	Ask workers to perform the task at their own pace.	Ask them to speak to you only when they are unable to proceed.
6	Observe silently.	Resist any temptation to explain or guide workers.
7	Speak only when the worker is unable to proceed.	Using a worksheet, make notes of the problem for each step or activity.
8	Look for signs of trouble or concern and make notes.	• Hesitation • Puzzled looks or sounds • Referring to earlier steps • Missing a step

3. Conclude the Observation

Formally end the test and thank your volunteers.

Steps for Concluding	
# **What To Do**	**How To Do It**
1 Remind workers that they participated in a test of *your instructions* and not their performance.	Say words to this effect: *"Because I am so familiar with this task, I might have easily overlooked steps that are important to someone who is experiencing it for the first time, as you just did. You helped me identify those areas and that made this a successful test."*
2 Discuss the task and take notes.	Ask an open-ended question such as: "W*hat was this experience like for you?"*
3 Ask workers for their completed worksheet.	• Make sure you can read their notes. • Ask about anything that is unclear. • Resist any urge to explain or disagree.
4 Thank workers for their assistance.	Say words to this effect: *"Thank you for helping me improve my instructions. You have contributed to the success of many people who will follow these guidelines."*

29. Revise and Release Your Instructions

After testing your instructions, revise them to eliminate problems reported by workers and problems you observed. This chapter explains the last five steps for completing your instructions.

1. Revise Your Instructions

The purpose of revising is to make your instructions clearer for your readers. Some tweaking is almost always required in first drafts. The notes you took when you tested your instructions (see Chapter 28: *Test Your Instructions*) indicate the changes you need to make. Rewrite any step that got one of the following reactions from a worker:

- A comment on a worker's observation worksheet
- A pause or hesitation
- A puzzled facial expression
- Mumbling or groaning
- Backtracking to read earlier steps
- A skipped step.

2. Determine Whether to Retest Your Instructions

If you made many revisions or rewrote an entire step, retest your revised instructions. Be sure to find a volunteer who is *un*familiar with the task. The workers who have already tested your instructions are not eligible.

Retest your instructions if any of the following conditions apply to the first test:

- Workers were unable to complete the task
- Workers missed a step
- Workers referred back to earlier steps
- Steps were missing
- Unnecessary steps were included
- Steps were out of order

After you retest your instructions, repeat the revision process.

3. Identify and Correct Grammatical Errors

After you revise your instructions, read them for grammatical errors or have someone else do this. Search for and correct the following:

- Misspelled words
- Incorrect sentence structure
- Improper punctuation
- Inconsistency in word use

Caution: Electronic spell-checking and grammar-checking devices do not recognize all grammatical errors!

4. Approve Final Copies

The best written instructions can be rendered useless by poor printing, reproduction or placement. Check a sample of the copies your readers will see. Make sure they are legible and clear. Look for:

- Distortions
- Font size changes (too small or too large)
- Over prints
- Missing text
- Unfavorable placement (instructions printed in unprotected places that can be easily damaged)
- Steps printed out of sequence

Note: This approval step will ensure that your readers get to see the effort and care you've put into writing excellent instructions!

5. Release Your Instructions

Congratulations! If you've followed the guidelines in this publication, you can be proud of your accomplishment as an Instruction Writer! You've written excellent instructions that will delight your readers!

Appendix A: Vague Expressions to Avoid

Vague expressions are imprecise references to attributes, characteristics, features and measurements. For example: How much is *a little*? What distance is *far*? Chapter 11, *Be Exact*, explains how to avoid using vague expressions. Following is a partial list:

a bit	etcetera (etc.)	nearly
a bunch	extra	not many
a large amount	fairly	on the order of
a little	far	practically
a lot	fat	quite
a moment	few	scarcely
a pinch	firm	several
a small amount	fuzzy	should
a tad	general	short
a while	hard	slightly
about	hardly	small
almost	hazy	smidgen
an adequate	heavy	soft
amount	hot	some
any	huge	sometime
approaching	immeasurable	somewhat
approximately	just about	soon after
around	late	soon before
attach	less	tall
barely	light	temporary
big	little	thereabouts
carefully	long	thin
closely	many	vast
cold	medium	very
dark	more	virtually
during	much	warm
early	narrowly	roughly

Appendix B: "Do" and "Degree" Words

"Do" words tell readers to perform a specific function or action. They describe both physical actions (movement) and mental actions (thinking). "Degree" words explain the intensity, speed or strength of the action. When used together, "do" and "degree" words answer this question for your readers:

> *"What <u>function</u> must I perform and at what <u>level</u> of exertion must I perform it?"*

For example:

> *"<u>Read</u> this publication <u>thoroughly</u> before you write instructions for the first time."*

Chapter 18, *Begin Action Sentences with "Do" and "Degree" Words,* provides guidelines for using these words.

<u>"Degree" Words</u>

<u>Intensity, Speed or Strength of an Action or Function</u>

accurately	forcefully	partially
briskly	frequently	professionally
carefully	fully	promptly
cautiously	gently	quickly
completely	gradually	rapidly
directly	heavily	slowly
easily	immediately	steadily
efficiently	lightly	swiftly
firmly	neatly	thoroughly

"Do" Words: Functions or Actions

Divide	Listen	Provide	Stamp
Draft	Locate	Pull	Start
Draw	Log	Push	State
Empty	Look	Raise	Stir
Enter	Make	Rank	Stitch
Erase	Maintain	Read	Stop
Establish	Measure	Recall	Strike
Estimate	Mince	Recite	Stroke
Examine	Monitor	Recognize	Subtract
Explain	Move	Record	Tabulate
Expose	Multiply	Relate	Talk
Face	Nail	Remember	Tap
File	Number	Remove	Taste
Focus	Observe	Repeat	Tell
Formulate	Obtain	Review	Think
Go	Order	Rub	Throw
Grab	Organize	Scan	Tilt
Grasp	Paint	Scroll	Touch
Group	Pause	See	Trace
Guess	Picture	Select	Transfer
Hit	Pin	Separate	Translate
Hold	Place	Sharpen	Tune
Identify	Plan	Show	Turn
Illustrate	Plug	Sketch	Twist
Imagine	Point	Slice	Type
Include	Post	Slide	Use
Indicate	Pound	Smash	Utilize
Inform	Pour	Smell	Wash
Inspect	Practice	Solve	Watch
Keep	Prepare	Specify	Whisper
Lift	Press	Spin	Wipe
List	Produce	Spread	Write

Appendix C: "Picture" Words

"Picture" words help readers identify, recall or imagine particular people, places and things. They include:

1. Words that name particular people, places, and things

2. Words that name features, attributes and characteristics of particular people, places and things

Chapter 19, *Use "Picture" Words to Describe People, Places and Things*, explains how to use picture words. Following are partial lists:

1. Words that Name People, Places and Things:

arrow	document	liquid	screwdriver
battery	electrician	manager	slot
bolt	frame	manual	specialist
book	handle	outlet	stepstool
box	hole	paper	surface
building	key	pen	switch
bulb	keyboard	plate	table
button	knob	plug	teacher
case	ladder	plumber	technologist
chair	lamp	point	theory
circle	lever	room	tube
desk	light	screen	wire

2. Words that Name Features, Attributes and Characteristics

black	copper	metal	round
blue	flaky	murky	soft
brass	flat	orange	square
bright	green	paper	square
clear	hard	rectangular	triangular

Appendix D: "Sound" Words

Words representing sounds help instruction readers determine whether things are working well. Sound words:

1. Imitate noises

2. Describe characteristics of sounds such as volume and intensity

   Chapter 20, *Describe Noises with "Sound" Words,* explains how to use sound words in instructions. Following are partial lists:

1. Noise Imitations

bong	creak	moan	smack
boom	ding	murmur	snap
buzz	dong	peal	splash
chime	fizz	ping	sputter
chirp	groan	pop	squeak
clang	growl	purr	squeal
clatter	hiss	rasp	swish
click	howl	rattle	thud
clink	hum	ring	tick
clunk	jingle	roar	tinkle
crackle	kerplunk	screech	twang
crash	knock	sizzle	whirr

2. Volumes, Intensities and Other Noise Characteristics

deafening	harsh	muted	shrill
deep	high-pitched	piercing	smooth
dull	hoarse	raucous	soft
grating	loud	roaring	soothing
gritty	melodious	rough	staccato
gruff	mellow	scratchy	thunderous
harmonious	muffled	sharp	tranquil

Appendix E: "Taste," "Touch" and "Smell" Words

"Taste" words describe flavors; "touch" words describe physical feelings; and "smell" words describe odors. These words can help readers determine whether things are working well when their task involves things that stimulate these senses. Following are partial lists:

"Taste" Words that Describe Flavors

bitter	salty	sugary	tart
bland	sour	sweet	vinegaryz
peppery	spicy	tangy	esty

"Touch" Words that Describe Physical Feelings

bumpy	greasy	pliable	soggy
coarse	hard	rigid	solid
cold	hot	rough	stiff
damp	jagged	sharp	stretchy
dry	limber	slimy	supple
firm	lumpy	slippery	taut
flexible	malleable	smooth	warm
frozen	oily	soft	wet

"Smell" Words that Describe Odors

burnt	mildew	pungent	rotten
flowery	moldy	rancid	scorched
foul	musty	rank	smoky

Appendix F: "On-Screen" Instructions

"On-screen" instructions are directions presented to readers via electronic technology. This refers to almost any non-paper medium, including:

- Computer monitor
- Video projection
- Television
- Hand-held communication devices

Computer-based, Internet-based, and Intranet-based instructions are presented to readers on a screen.

The guidelines in this publication apply to instructions written on hard-copy (paper) as well as in electronic technology. This appendix includes three additional guidelines that apply to electronically-delivered instructions.

1. Write Electronically-Delivered Instructions in the Same Way

People learn the same way from electronic media as they do from books and other paper documents. The use of technology may or may not enhance learning for some readers. Follow the guidelines in this publication for writing instructions regardless of the technology you use.

2. Adapt for Limited Visual Space

There is usually less viewing area on a screen-page than on a paper-page. Avoid causing your readers to have to scroll up or down to read a necessary part of an instruction or to remember what was presented on a previous screen. Present your instructions in such a way that all of the information your readers need to complete a step or activity appears on a single screen-page. Do this even if your instructions are accompanied by audio. Follow these guidelines:

- Present a complete step or subordinate activity on a single on-screen page.

- Present multiple steps on an on-screen page when they fit.

- Repeat instructions when they must be remembered from an earlier step.

Note: Information Technologists prefer to list information only once to save data-storage space. Disregard this constraint and repeat information if it will simplify your readers' task.

3. Use the Full Capability of Your Technology

Animated video, sound and color are readily available in electronic media. These features can make your readers' job easier or harder, depending on how they are used. In addition to the information provided in Chapter 24, *Illustrate Your Instructions*, following are a few tips that apply when using electronic technology:

a. Provide instructions about how to use the technology to operate, activate or view your illustrations.

b. Make audio instructions optional at your readers' discretion. Audio may be disruptive to others in shared environments.

c. Use highly contrasting colors to make text easy to read.

d. Design animated illustrations to demonstrate how to perform important or especially difficult functions.

e. Insert long pauses. Explain only one step or activity at a time in audio and animated video instructions.

f. Provide the capability for your readers to print a paper copy of the text of your instructions.

Make sure your illustrations are important to completing the task rather than just for entertainment

Breinigsville, PA USA
12 January 2011
253164BV00004B/204/P